Lost and Found

Written and Illustrated by

Diane Simon

Lost and Found

Library of Congress
Cataloging in Publication Data

ISBN 978-1-60880-605-8

Proudly manufactured in the United States of America by

Roops Mill Publishing
Westminster, Maryland

I am dedicating this book to my grandchildren—Keira, Alyssa, Wylie, and Lucas. They are a constant source of inspiration for me. I watch them navigating a world that presents challenging opportunities and choices every day. I hope my little story will encourage children and their parents to discuss ways we can all bring more kindness into our everyday lives.

It is a big job being "a most loved" toy. It is an all-day affair and can even keep you up at night.

2Bunny knew all about this; 2Bunny was Lissie's most favorite toy. Everywhere Lissie went, 2Bunny went, too. Maybe that is how he got his name.

One Friday morning, 2Bunny woke up a little bored. *Just another day*, he thought. Friday meant grocery shopping—*BORING!*

I could use a change, he thought. How about an adventure? As they entered the store he began to think, *probably no adventure for me today*. So he settled down for a little nap.

Shopping went as usual and then the unthinkable happened! As Mom, big sister Kiki, and Lissie left the store, 2Bunny was left behind in the cart.

A new family, Mr. and Mrs. Shrewburt, entered the store in a big hurry. They grabbed a cart and did not see 2Bunny sleeping quietly at the bottom. They were in a big hurry because in exactly one hour their three hungry grandsons would be arriving for lunch.

They flew through the aisles dropping piles of snacks on a sleeping 2Bunny. Soon only one small foot stuck out. "What's this?" asked Mrs. Shrewburt as she spotted the foot and uncovered the sleeping 2Bunny.

As 2Bunny opened his eyes, his whole world was turned upside down. He stared up at Mrs. Shrewburt's face wondering, *where are Lissie and Mom and Kiki? Are they hiding, or is this the beginning of an adventure?*

"Yuk," declared Mrs. Shrewburt as she turned him around by his tail! "This is a very dirty toy covered in yucky spots," she said with disgust.

2Bunny was confused; he knew exactly how he got his spots. One day Lissie had pointed to his spots and Grandma picked him up to take a closer look. "Just what I thought," she said. "He has Love spots."

"Is that bad?" asked Lissie.

"Oh, no," said Grandma. "They come from lots of hugs." She would say the more love spots you have the more you are loved. He wondered why didn't this lady know that.

Mr. Shrewburt thought 2Bunny was cute. He smiled at 2Bunny and said, "I bet one of our grandsons would love to have him."

"Never," cried Mrs. Shrewburt and tossed him quickly away.

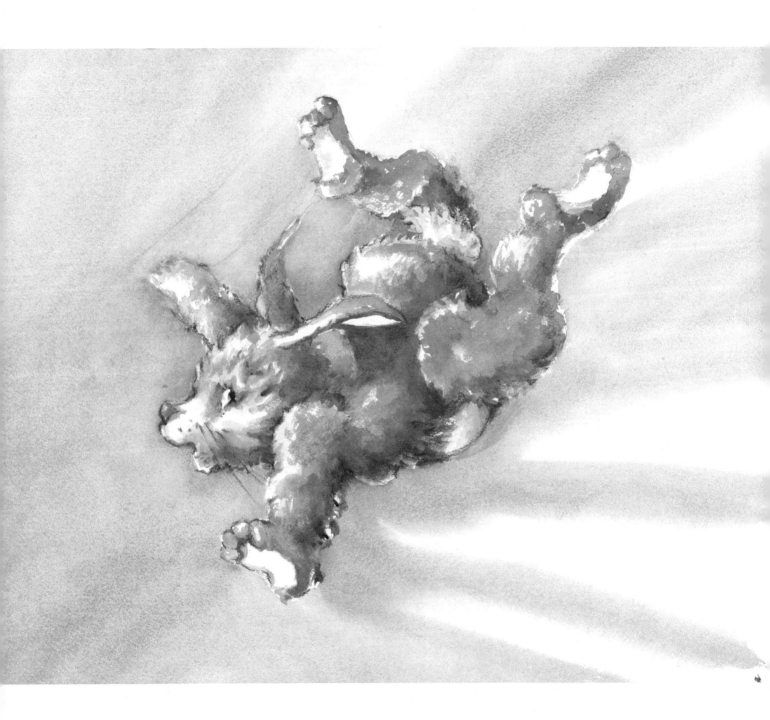

6

2Bunny went sailing through the air and I know it's hard to believe but he landed right into another shopping cart! A Dad and his two sons never saw 2Bunny land right on top of their box of chocolate cupcakes.

Dad was busy talking to a grocery clerk when the younger boy spotted him. "Look, it's Peter Rabbit."

"That is NOT Peter Rabbit," said his older brother as he quickly took him away. He took a closer look and said, "We have discovered a spy. Look how fat he is. He sneaks into peoples' grocery carts spying out their best treats, then steals them away."

With that, he took off his shoe and a sock and tied the sock securely around 2Bunny's eyes. "He can't see our treats, he can't steal our treats, and he is out of here," cried the older brother and tossed him high in the air.

As 2Bunny sailed into the air the little brother felt sad. "I wanted to give him a cupcake. I like to share."

So this is my adventure, thought 2Bunny as he flew
through the air. It was kind of special to be mistaken for
a spy. However, being called fat was not what he wanted
to hear. In fact, he began to think how nice it would be
to be called by his real name 2Bunny.

I know it's very hard to believe, but 2Bunny sailed right into another shopping cart!

Two very close friends, Abby and Felicia, were shopping for cookie supplies. They planned to have a yard sale and sell cookies, hoping to attract more customers.

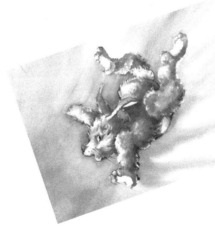

10

Felicia was the first to spot him- sprawled on top of the chocolate chips. *Where did he come from!* She thought. Some small child must have lost their bunny.

Abby saw him, too, and quickly grabbed him, removing the sock from his eyes. As 2Bunny stared back, she took a closer look and said, "Kind of dirty, but I think we can sell him at our yard sale. We might even get two dollars for him, but what do you think?"

Felicia said, "I think he might belong to some little kid who might be missing him a lot. We should try to find his owner."

Abby was determined to sell him, but Felicia suddenly got an idea. She reached into her pocket and pulled out four dollars.

"Here you go—SOLD for twice your asking price." Then with no one noticing, as they left the store, she dropped 2Bunny into an empty shopping cart, hoping his real owner would find him.

2Bunny lay quietly in the bottom of the cart. He began to truly miss Lissie and wondered when this adventure would be over. He also began to wonder what he was worth. Two dollars?

Then one of his favorite memories came to mind. Every night Lissie's Dad would come into her bedroom at bedtime. He would bend down and kiss Lissie and point to 2Bunny and say, "Who is this?"

Lissie would laugh and say, "Daddy you know who this is!"

"Tell me," he would say with his eyes wide with curiosity.

"It's 2Bunny, my bestest friend!"

Then Daddy would bend over and give 2Bunny a kiss, saying with a smile, "Well, then he must be priceless." 2Bunny didn't know what priceless meant, but it sounded like more than two dollars.

Just as Abby and Felicia were leaving the store, Mom, Kiki, and Lissie were returning. It did not take long for Lissie to miss 2Bunny. They had turned around in the car and came back as quickly as they could.

Mom was the first to see him lying in the bottom of the cart. "Look, it's 2Bunny—he's right where we left him," she cried with relief.

"I missed you so much, my bestest friend," sobbed Lissie.

"Let's bake a cake and have a 2Bunny celebration," called out Kiki.

I can tell you one thing for sure: 2Bunny might look the same way on the outside, but only he knew how different he felt on the inside. Yes, 2Bunny had his adventure and now he knew that the best adventure of all is sharing love.

15

CPSIA information can be obtained
at www.ICGtesting.com
Printed in the USA
BVHW020007130621
609328BV00001B/6